⎡n Enniskillen in 1968. He has been ⎿ʜsʟ ᴄ ⎿ennessy Award and placed in The ⎿anagh Prize and The New Writer Poetry Prize. He was Writer-in-Residence in Fermanagh in 2002 and he lectured in Traditions at Poets' House from 2000 to 2004. He holds an MA with Distinction in Creative Writing from Lancaster University and his debut collection, *At The Waters' Clearing* (Flambard/Black Mountain Press, 2001) received widespread critical acclaim. He also co-edited *Breaking the Skin* (Black Mountain Press, 2002), an anthology of new Irish poets. He is currently completing a PhD.

By the same author

Poetry
At the Waters' Clearing

Co-Editor
Breaking the Skin

SONGS FOR NO VOICES

SONGS FOR NO VOICES

NIGEL McLOUGHLIN

LAGAN PRESS
BELFAST
2004

Acknowledgements

The publishers wish to acknowledge the following magazines and broadcasting media in which some of these poems have previously appeared: *Abraxas, Acumen, Agenda, Black Mountain Review, Books Ireland, The Brobdingnagian Times, Burning Bush, Cutting Teeth, Electric Acorn, Envoi, Equinox, Faultline (USA), Fabric, Fire, Hybrid, InCognito, The Journal of Irish Studies (Japan), The New Writer, Noises From The Isle, Orbis, Outposts, Poetry Monthly, Radio Foyle, Radio Ulster, Ropes, Sepia, The Shop, South, The Sunday Tribune, Thunder Sandwich* and *Ulster Tatler.*

The publisher also wish to acknowledge the editors of the following anthologies in which some of these poems have previously appeared: *Breaking the Skin* (Black Mountain Press) and *Modern Poets of Europe* (Spiny Babbler Press, Nepal).

Published by
Lagan Press
Unit 11
1A Bryson Street
Belfast BT5 4ES
e-mail: lagan-press@e-books.org.uk
web: lagan-press.org.uk

ARTS
COUNCIL
of Northern Ireland

ISBN: 1 904652 15 8
Author: McLoughlin, Nigel
Title: Songs For No Voices
2004

Set in Sabon
Cover: *Última Oração* (1999) by Luis Athouguia
(reproduced courtesy of the artist)
Design: December
Printed by Easyprint, Belfast

This book is dedicated to my wife, Teresa,
with all my love,
for putting up with a poet.

Contents

The Vase
for Teresa

I have never been one for buying flowers:
you bought your own and brought them back—
tiny yellow buds that floated in a sea of flock.
The sugared water you put in kept them fresh
and after a few days their heads opened.
Fold after fold of yellow petals spilled
above the neck of an off-white vase.

I had never noticed it, the vase I mean,
I disregarded it daily as it sat slightly
to the left and a touch behind the television.
But now as each set of flowers pass their best
and end up in the bin, it sits in the room like a gap
or staring at me as a stranger might,
ushering me out to buy more yellow roses.

Opus to the Manifest

I will write a stone book, a weight
to break the entropy of silence;
use a quote from *Das Kapital*
to seal my head, like a draught excluder,
erect no entry signs to the winds of change.

I will look at the world through a Moorish window,
see Leopold of Austria in his last waltz,
whip it up in a mix of words and put it down
in writing. I will taste nothing. I will be tasteless.

I will sign my life away in lawsuits,
live and die an opulent graveyard of words,
drag the living shards of thought to the dark.

I will offer a dead man's manifesto:
a magnum opus of nonsense.

I will offer Art.

Songs For No Voices

Forty Shades of Fuchsia

I could show you three pictures from an old man's head.
I could show you that they lasted him a lifetime.
I could show you the last tree on an island
and the men breaking their boats to bury their dead.
I could show you a sky at evening.
I could show you forty shades of fuchsia.

I could show you bodies wasting into long shadows.
I could show you men dropping where they worked.
I could show you the road to nowhere
and where they say there is hungry grass.
I could show you a field of wild flowers.
I could show you forty shades of fuchsia.

I could show you a son standing over his father.
I could show you the grip slackening on his arm.
I could show you the plea in his eyes at his last words:
'Ná bí ag briseadh baidí ar bith domsa.'
I could show you a host of boats at sail.
I could show you forty shades of fuchsia.

Half Remembered

Alone in the dark
a little boy lies incoherent;
his shivering body colder
than any corpse.
Sweat pours out like agony
but cannot cool
the engulfing fever's burn.

Distantly, he can hear
an opening door
and familiar footsteps pace
towards him like a heartbeat.
A soothing hand quells
the fire in his head
and a few soft words are
murmured low till sleep.
Descending in a kiss,
peace embraces him;
blanketing his pain—

and somewhere in the darkness
a fever breaks.

Elegy

We stripped and burned the little bridge
each Hallowe'en; left just enough
to ford our way to school.
We walked across ice in winter
till one fell in and drowned.

The contraband fireworks we cut
from the rushes, once dried
were paraffin-dipped and set *a'lou*.
We sent them thrumming from bows
flame-arching back to the lough.

Walking where the sallies
bent to water every summer
by lough and wall, we dandered
slow, as though sent to cut
a rod for our own beating.

The kingfisher and the heron which stood
sentinel, kept nix to our misdemeanours,
are gone leaving the lone banshee
curlew to lament our punishment,
to ululate our passing, and theirs.

Polishing the Stones

About halfway through the work, when time
came to rest and eat, he'd lead us up
to the standing stones that lay flat out
in the hillside sun. And measured out in mugs
of tea, sandwiches and hard-boiled eggs,
he'd tell the tallest tales, with juicy details,
just the right amount of spice. They were always
balanced delicately on the border of believable.

And when the hour was up, he'd lift his cup
and drain it down to the leaves and lick
his lips and rise to walk back down the hill.
A backward look, a smile, and he'd say:
'I think we've polished them stones about enough.'
But of course, that was the whole trick.

Late Snow

Drunk, we brushed away the years,
into snow that lay knee deep,
soft as talcum, dry as powdered bone.
Three of us, children,
numb-fingering snowballs into ice.
We pelted ears already singing from
the cold. Faces shaded beetroot and maroon.

Tomorrow, we'll grow up again
to trudge respectably through slush,
but tonight, while the trees are
all moon-feathered, the hills are
daylight bright and fluorescence
is blinding off the snow,
tonight, one last time, we'll deflower
the virgin of our imaginations.

Voodoo

Once, I murdered him,
the man who was my double:
I drank until his liver burst,
smoked until his lungs gave out,
left every woman he ever loved.
It broke his heart in the end,
left him suicidal, killed him.
But I emerged laughing
from the wreckage of his years
and now I see, smiling
in the mirror of his cold eyes,
cold eyes.

Names

You turned up again,
in another man's story.
He called you slapper,
he called you whore,
he called you 'Juliet'.

Yet I recognised you
from your missing trigger
finger, left years ago on
a Belfast barricade
like an apology.

He filled in your history—
the pregnancy, the whoring,
the suspicion of HIV,
how life was severed from you
numb-quick as amputation.

All this narrated third person.
But I knew you before all that,
when you were beautiful,
and I called you by
an older, closer name.

Reinventing the Light Bulb

The mouth gapes at the dark
inside it, flying in filaments
circling in like paranoia,
breaking like a virus in the cell
of the head, shining out from a black
ecstasy of terror.
                    Soon, you think,
it has to burn out and pop, shattering
the brush-stroke tension,
forcing outward in a scream
to batter the walls of the gallery;
become the colour of total extinction
consuming itself in an island of light.

Song For No Voices

All the words I loved are gone,
leaving me, mouth stopped,
with this slack tongue,
my jaw locked with rigor.
There are things left unsaid,
of course, there always are,
on one side or the other.

But I remember how my
outstretched arm would circle
the nape of your neck,
your head lolling forward
full of sleep, the sweat
on the curls below your jaw,
a breast-brush on my thumb
that timed your breathing.

I remember feeling the foetus stir
beneath your skin, under my limp
hanging hand, how your turning
legs encircled mine, hot tears
on my cheek and warm kisses.
It's these things I'm willing you
to remember, willing you to forget.

What's left to say? I left
too quick, too quick, my love,
like the turn of a kiss; left you
to batten down your grief with nails;
give sorrow to the warm wood and
tell our child, that I never knew,
I never knew.

Keepsake

For years she kept it
in a matchbox,
a lock of hair
held at one end
with red elastic.

She took it out
once a year
examining, fingering
the colour change
until it became
the colour of her own.

Yet something stayed
flaming in that matchbox,
burnt into her memory—
wordless and distant
as her eyes.

A Shadow of Ghosts

The dawn flecks the sky
hot as a bridal blush;
and a translucent mist
hovers, like a lover's breath,
above the water.
I sit alone at my window
and watch the sunrise.

The air cools, dancing on my skin
like the afterglow of you,
and my mind is haunted;
fixed by feelings of love, regret
and old mistakes.
The past leaves with the night—
day is still a future away.

But here in the half-light
it is only the delicate
and the tender that exist;
pure as mist upon the water;
untameable as fires in the sky
and bodies are just shadows of ghosts
as spirits kiss.

In Other Words

I can hear it under the silences
of trees: roots growing around rock,
around bone, fingering through
territories as alien as burial places.
From the bank that looms outside
my kitchen window, dripping seaward
to a strand, half land, half water,
I feel it coursing: this urge to stay.

But how can I, a maker of poems,
short works; a drifter from subject
to subject, constant as the tide
I sleep to, rise to; shored in
a short time between two peninsulas,
how can I stay put, defy my nature
when I am used to love affairs
short, complete in themselves, left?

Still I have this urge not to go;
a positive among all my negatives.
Normally, I stay out of complacency,
through being tired of shape-shifting,
as an exercise in re-charging,
but this time it's different, it is words
I can barely form, words my mouth
gapes at, my tongue trips over.

Words my heart has found music to
for the first time. Words that drip
water from teeth to a parched tongue,
that taste of metal, sharp and biting
in the throat. Words that come to me
from somewhere alien or imagined:
Tá mé i ngrá léi.
I still haven't decided what they mean.

Funeral Music

Pipe

Remember that grinding action
as he twists the knife into his palm;
chips, screws and gradually softens
the block of *Old Warhorse Walnut Plug*
in that brown hand of his, and its heart
as hard as the barrel of his pipe.

Remember how he holds the pipe
in his mouth as he mixes his mortar,
grips it occasionally in that claggy mitt,
narrows an eye, and gently tamps
his plug into the barrel just loose enough
to suck great teeth-gritting lungfuls back.

Remember how the smoke is released
with a smile from the prison of his body,
how breath will come wriggling between
the bars of his teeth, find the air and dissipate.
He'll turn back to his work so you won't see
the plougher that wracks him, the rusty spit.

Dusk, Lough Erne

Slate-blue clouds bedded in vermilion
break the darkness, hover in the mist.
These are the old places, names
like soft metal oozings rust in silence.

Skeletal shadows, silk-grey-cast
on the lake's glacier warp and tangle
in the cut-glass turning of a day,
are water-swallowed into night's ghosting.

A bird whispers, throaty as guttural.
A mystery of colour turns rose to gold
softly like a final lullaby chorus.
The sun relaxes, drowns in sounds:

hushed rustles, peeps and twitters
and from under the silent places,
eyes on the back of my neck—
banished watchers stationed

like old ghosts, between the wood
and the bark of trees long felled.

An Trá Bhán

My feet already know the way
through the whispering recesses
that form the capillaries of this
inner country. As though walking
home on radar, late, along bedding
planes and pavements; these synaptic
roads are shadowlands of a landscape
more alien than imagined.

I am drawn here, sure-footed, agile,
across borders, into tunnels, under walls,
the air is catgut taut and silence is
shredding frost into the misty sublimation
that is sleep. And I become a child
again, climbing karsts and clacking
off pebbles, become beached here
where the stepping stones melt into cliffs.

The waves foam around the blowhole like
rabid dogs and I can go no further, but
I can see the sea blanket and uncover
beaches further off, in time with my
hard breathing. It's as though I stand
here as I've always stood, ready
to step off, to fall into the boiling
under overhangs that threatens
to tear down the world.

Cut Up

Silver screams lost in a cloud dungeon
church this crimson gloom to sunrise,
shiver the mist that is necking our room.

Say: 'nightmare' and I rattle like a mirror,
moon all the spider night to seize a storm-
ghost, the black angel of your blood.

Bury this candle breath coffin dark, down
here, where we empty tears with cold velvet;
come make a grave—haunt me if I cry.

Baile an Easa

She likes to go walking late at night
and the hooded figure that I pass
on the road might well be hers.

The laughing murders of crows amass
and almost break the branches
with dead weight. Burning sky blackens

into monochrome. The middle ground
becomes a series of grey shades.
Gorse burns. The moon drips, a rheumy

eye through sackcloth, gibbous, changing
like the pupil of a cat. It darkens
off wet roofs where the glint of bulbs

are moons in windows. The sodium light
yellows everything: the tree, the house,
the pillar of the road. Crossed by beams

of a car, animal eyes redden in the night.
The moon has become a bull's eye,
reddening in Taurus, unsilencing this place,

loosing the hush and rush that named it
once. The back of my neck quickens,
nerves goosepimple, hair stands. I feel

shadows cross where there is no light.

At Trory Point

By glitter-gold of water-sun
sounds, all birdsong and motors;
lazy silences and rest.
An island, cut out of sky and water,
jutting from a stone pier.
Reed-ripple of water lapping
on stone. The squeal of children
playing; brightening in the evening.
Sun sinks. Sky whitens in the dusk.

Her Face

I saw her face in the local paper,
one hundred years old. Her skull
barely skimmed with skin
impaled on that frail frame,
thin lipped; enduring.

The fight still lit her eyes
though now they lay sunken
in the shadows of too many years.
Hair blown back like one
facing into wind; defiant,

she carried the lines of private
jokes, shared now only with the dead;
but her contented smile, the way it
gently filled her face from the inside;
that was beautiful, proud, complete.

Cattle Shed

The cattle lowed their way between the stones
of this old shed where they were herded daily
from grass to gate, until the day he fell dead
between two horses pulling a rusty thresher
up the field. Neighbours lifted him, carried him
inside and laid him out across the kitchen table.

That was forty years ago and grass grows high
around the shed. Stones have tumbled from
the roofbar, scattered to the ground and still
cattle nose around while a stranger tends the land.
The grass, the field have gathered his grave in
and death has held him tight in open hands.

The Find

It was getting on for evening when I found them
glistening and solid under the cracked roof:
eggs, green as the gloom in the ruin,
nested into a bundle of old newspaper,
lying on a rusted bed.
                        I searched
the rafters, scanning for a wing-beat,
cocking my ear for a chirp.
I knew I shouldn't interfere with the nest
and was making to retreat when something
blacker than old red lead and softer than stone
caught my eye in the grate.
                        Lifting it,
I held the sooty, still-warm corpse
and felt for a beat or breath among
its bony softness. Finding none,
I touched the eggs.
                        They were cold
as glass in my hand as I cupped them out
into the light. I washed the bird in ditch-water
and the feathers blazed. I left the bird, the eggs,
the nest, like an offering on the warm ground.
Next day I found all of them gone.

Funeral Music

The old man down the road is a tree:
his limbs are twisted, knotted, slim
and his head is a crow's nest wintered
in the tangle of his hair.

A bark-brown coat rumples his trunk
but no sap rises through the dark
veins clotted in his hands. Years
are storms to him, a rage

and howl of wind, a clash and batter
of rain and lightning, sending coursing
through his wood, a symphony of decay,
his funeral music.

A Present From Pompeii

Shocked in a shell-
shaped paperweight,
a sea scene, simplified
to a sea horse, stones,
starfish, weeds, shells.

A manufactured memory,
a lightweight, imitation Pompeii,
where pumice lovers fused
and real life was ashed out,
frozen for the future.

The sea horse swims forward
as if wanting to be asked:
what Vesuvius poured over,
entombed him under glass,
painted his background black?

Crows

Glaucous ruptures of air
turn impossibly on updrafts,
skim imminent ground.

The unlucky plummet,
become a bolus of feather
and bone, grow maggoty with life.

Tragedy is beautiful
from the outside.
Death is sweet
as silence in the throat.

Bat

Out of the briar tangle
I felt your loose needle
bone between my finger
and my thumb, the bag
of fur, the skitter of wings.

My grip adjusted, hemmed
you in, fast in my fist.
I saw the supersonic squeal
of your mouth; a tissue
creature unpulsing all
other vital signs, cold
as winter in my grip.

My arm extends,
fingers flex like petals,
sudden to the moon.
I watch you loop
and circle freedom,
alive and winging it.

Epicedium
i.m. James McLoughlin

At four years old I'd turn up and stand and watch the line
shoot, a yard at a time, into a perfect circle in the box,
how you'd lash hooks with finger twists too quick
    to be a knot.
When you sat, a cross-legged magician, mending nets,
all wrists and teeth that somehow missed the flying needle,

I'd let fly with a head-full of questions. You'd answer
with a wink and a nod to Ned or Paul and I'd believe you,
for I knew you knew all the green secrets of the fish,
every cold vector of the lough, the shallows and the depths,
where all the black eels hid and the hook-jawed,
    monstrous pike.

Always, you'd take me in and guide my hand slowly through
the making of a knot, again and again, until I'd get it right,
or show me how to patch a broken net before you'd go.
And I'd watch you all down the road, making for the lough,
where I knew your boat was waiting and ready for the water.

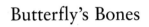

Butterfly's Bones

A New Language

I can hear it in my voice,
like a cold or laryngitis;
a new dis-ease—ceasefire.
A broken flow of words
shyly stammered by
an adolescent, uncomfortable
with my new tone.

An alien voice forced
down familiar throats;
it sounds like ice breaking,
or the voices of my generation,
trying, self-consciously,
to circumnavigate this
new language of peace.

The Morning After

A sackcloth morning sky
is looming through my window,
provoking me into waking.

I can smell the petrol,
feel the soaking of the rags
as flames taste the darkening air.

I can see the beacons burning
their warnings from the hills,
feel each coffin shouldered.

The day comes too late,
too late the tears,
too late the penitent ashes.

Butterfly's Bones

Mostly, they are hardly noticed
for they are too small or soft
to demand notice. They seem
to hide, shying from the gaze,
shrinking from touch. Their recoil
is instinctive. Yet their small voices
roaring from the invisible are enough
to turn or cock a head like scent
in the breeze or an aftertaste.

Mostly, we don't look hard enough
or tight enough to see them,
our forkèd-ways vision dims
them to denials, myths, lies.
Yet God is full of them, these
tiny poems, and if we could only
tune ourselves to hear the rattle
that photons make, taste heat
on the moving air, find the subtle
scent of iron, see the spinning
electron dance everywhere
and nowhere simultaneously,

or if we could touch, gently,
gently, the insignificant
butterfly's bones, then maybe,
maybe we'd understand,
as children do, the last faint
and distant echoes of the voice
of our once-thundering God.

In the House

Errigal is violet with snow and light
and the falling air drags smoke down
from chimneys to slacken at eaves.

Silence blackens like the fire back
where I pace my grate impatient
for kindling. I cold-shoulder

the January air to the far poles
of the house with fire, drive
blocks of wood into embers. Light

catches my eye from the white
night outside like a face
at my window. I startle briefly.

Without the wind's low murmur
it's easy to be lonely. Too lazy
to trek to the car, I settle

for the kettle and TV, the pub
attracts me less these days,
I seldom show my face. Now

it's bitter out, even though it's just
an inch or two of snow. The log-pile
across the yard is frozen, but I go,

return, arms full, sliding on the hard
patch at the door. Opening it, I hear
the mobile ringing. I dump the logs

in the wood-box, jump across the chair
and grab and answer just in time.
'Hello,' you say, 'Where are you?'

Without thinking, I find myself saying
'I'm at home.'

Man of the People

Powers straight up, chasers by glasses,
fifteen rounds and he's lethal:
making passes, building towers
of glass, jarring the bouncers,
clinging to counters, steeple-
jacking his way up the stool.

He's hurled out on the street,
crass and mad, flat on his back
and plastered. He struggles up,
aims a kick at the door,
craving more drink, thick
with bad humour. He falls
on his arse. Garda Síochána
patrolling the corner decide
to come over.

They begin to frogmarch him
back to the station.
He's giving them hell,
shouting the odds at the top
of his lungs: he knows his rights.
It's Saturday night, just out for the fun
—a man of the people—meaning no harm.
And so they escort him,
one either arm.

Where is he living?
He's not bloody telling—
the wife'll just kill him—
and so he ends up
locked in a cell.

He wakes up unwell,
fifteen pints drier
and skint.

Poitín Maker

Elfin renegade in the hill, turnkey
to the secrets of the worm,
maker of good mash, lighter of fires
under stills. Consistent in his humour
as his whiskey, a man who can speak
volumes with a wink and a smile;
who avoids conversation like excise.

But underneath all his tight-lipped
bargaining, there is a total surety
of all the heart's distillings,
drilling through copper,
dripping off tongues.
See it burning in his eyes,
clear blue, like flame.

Orders

Nature inveigles each successive
turning of the sod, ploughs men
to the ground; calls the seed, fruit.
Turning, turning, slow as the world,

life in time-lapse; snapshots
run together; accelerating to an end;
re-quickening. Purpose is change;
bending, bending, wide as a river.

Age melts its way, weathering one
into the other. All the tenses marry
in the end, returning somehow unnoticed,
creeping, creeping, on all-fours like a child.

The Old Way

Leaning over like a carrion crow,
mumbling prayers for the saving
of his soul, having convinced the old man
at last that the church's need
is greater than his own, a solemn
eye cast upon the pen, he'll
watch him sign. And soon,
having got from him the lease,
they'll nail the old man down
and covered up in earth he'll
rest in peace.

First Sense

Since the womb first sparked
our flesh awake, we've sensed
the grave: its dark sweet smell;
the rattling spade and heavy spit
of sponging sod on ground well watered.
We've always known it totally:

the coarse sound of rooks creaking
on the overburdened branches;
the taste of well-wormed cattle
fed on those same pastures;
the weight of warm wood's strain
and the heat of crumbling turf's decay.

But now the storm has ceased
the freshening air wafts out
the smell of hay after rain,
singing through the sinuses like freedom
and in the distance a cricket and
a bird sing a drowsy sun awake.

A Lumen Spento

Between the hoarfrost and the trembling air
I woke, sweating out a Bhopal dream.
I can see it as through my window, congealing;
hanging like a cloud stilling the air,
a picture, flickering out an industry of sorrow.
How hard they must have prayed and cried
for death, release or simple asphyxia.
After nearly twenty years they're crying, praying still.

From the ground below, an earth-strong voice
is calling out, pleading recognition, rest.
Here they know who digs the graves when all
the gravediggers are dead; how many rotted
in the sun. They know the gas-filled trench
with an intimacy long-since named indecent.
Above all they know how deep the darkness is,
when all the lights have, finally, been extinguished.

The Aistriúchán Coat

I'll Call No Help
from the Irish of Aogan Ó Rathaille

I'll call no help till I'm crushed to my coffin,
by all accounts, it wouldn't aid me if I did!
Our cornerstone, the strong-handed seed of Eoghan
lies with veins flayed and his strength ebbing.

Waves rattle the brain, the prime hope is gone,
there's a void in the plexus, the bowels impaled.
Our land, our shelter, our woods and our plains
are pennethed out by the hoard from Dover.

The Shannon, the Liffey, the musical Lee struck dumb
with the Barrow, Nuir, Suir and the Boyne;
the sides of Lough Derg and the great wave of Tóim
run red since the Knave has stripped the crowned King.

My war cry continues, a spate of spilled tears
and tragedy tilts the scale of the mind,
and the music I hear as I wander the roads
is the squeal of the pig that cannot be stuck.

Ah, hero of Rinn and Cill and Eoghanacht country,
your belly is slack from want and neglect,
and a hawk holds the land, racks it with rent,
shows favour to no-one, not even his own.

Because of the ruin of our royal line
sweat harrows the furrows of my head in grief,
becoming a source to send boiling streams
to the river that flows from Truipeall to Youghal.

I'll end it all here—for my last agony comes, now
the dragons are sundered from the Laune to the Lee
and I'll share my grave with the chief that I loved
and kings my kin served before the Passion of Christ.

A Father's Lament
from the Irish of Séan Ó Muiríosa

If, tomorrow, you're in Tuar an Fhíona
walk around to the yellow hill,
where men are fair and so respectful
and all the ladies fond of you.
And if they ask who you belong to,
ah, Séan Ó Muiríosa's lovely daughter,
tell them, softly, who you are.

Tomorrow you'll sleep in a bed made for you
and you'll have to root and dig no more,
for there men's hands do not grow tired,
you'll be bedded down in daylight
and never want for food nor clothes.

I would have given you gold and silver,
would have given you a field of cows,
and brought home your marriage bed
but in the cold dark Fort of Glory
you chose to lay your head instead.

Fever

from the Irish of Séan Ó Ríordáin

These mountains of bed are so high,
the plain in the centre is burning
and it's a far-flung flight to the floor.
    It seems that it's miles and miles distant:
    that world of sitting and standing.

I'm stuck in a state of bed linen
where a chair is vague in my memory.
    Ages ago I was walking,
    standing as high as a window,
    now I'm a plateau in this bed.

On the wall there's a picture expanding
and its frame slowly drips down the wall
and a weak faith like mine cannot stop it.
    I feel it close in all around me,
    feel the whole world in its fall.

A townland descends from the sky,
there's a parish at the tip of my finger,
how easy to grasp at the church.
    There are cows on the road to the north
    but the cows of forever are moving.

Washing the Corpse
from the German of Rainer Maria Rilke

They had grown used to him. But after
the kitchen lamp was lit and burned
restlessly in a dark draught, the stranger
was stranger still. They washed his neck,

and since they did not know his story,
they lied another to take its place
and kept on washing. One had to cough
and left the heavy vinegar sponge

lying on his face. This gave the second
time to rest. Drips fell from the hard
scrubbing-brush, while the horror of his
contorted hand tried to make the whole
house aware that he was no longer thirsty.

And he made it known. With short
embarrassed coughing they began
to work more hurriedly, so that
across the wallpaper's muted pattern,

their crooked shadows tossed and turned
as in a net, until the washing ended.
The pitiless night was framed in the uncurtained
window. And one without a name lay there
clean and naked and issued orders.

Night Wrestling
from the Irish of Áine Ní Ghlinn

There are nights my fingers slip to you
to find only a pillow soaked with tears,
her bony fingers running through your hair.

There are times I think I know her,
see her bones outstretched beside you,
cold lips sucking at your dream.

There are times I dream a cold November,
rain lashing your black tie,
your starched eyes above a pallid collar.

I've felt you turn to smooth her hair
and empty contact wake you as
your fingers drop through air.

I feel them coming for me now
but I clamp shut my eyes. I
will not wrestle with the dead.

She Was Faithless
from the Irish of Seán Ó Ríordáin

The old Lee entreats eastward,
   a deliberate prayer,
as a yellow autumn moon is printed
   in the silent spread
of stars and daylight is
   swooning in crimson.
A limp pup sprawls
   sluggish, sleeping.
If I could douse my heart
   in the red Lee
it would shatter banks
   like demons.
If I sent skyward my rage,
   my thoughts,
the storm would break
   and screaming devils
would spit venom at the moon
   and crap lightning.
The sun that stole daylight
   would be forced
to return and thwart the dark
   and broadcast
Hell's iniquity, blinding
   the heavens.
If I were to whisper one sigh
   of my unspeakable sorrow
in the ear of the sleeping pup
   he would race
to hunt dark caverns
   hounding out the blood
of the whisper that poisoned
   his heart as he slept.
Brooding, I bear it,
   chant it everywhere,
this mantra:
   she was faithless.

The Rider's Reproach
from the Irish of Aodh Mac Gabhráin

Gods curse you to hell, in the name
of my father! Fuck off out of my sight!
And be sick for a year, if not longer,
for you've cost me my woman tonight!

You stupid, idle, lump of oul' dog food,
such a shameless act to have done!
To drop me in front of my loved one
head first in a great pile of dung!

May death spasms grip you this evening!
And may your arse forever be cursed!
And ravens pluck your eyes from the sockets,
you devil's own hoor of the haunch!

May a nail be driven up through your foot!
and your tail be cut off to make fiddles!
And lightning shoot right up your butt!
And your backbone be slashed up and griddled!

Not a mouthful of grass, you glue-boiler,
will you get, nor one grain of corn,
nor never taste one drop of water,
till you wilt from the thirst that comes on!

May your right leg take out with its ball joint
a slab from the round of your hip!
A bolt up the arse might just wake you!
Didn't you see her at the window, you shit?

The Servant
from the Irish of Dáibhí Ó Bruadair

She's barren and bony, a nosy oul' shrew
who refused me a drink an' me throat like a bone.
A pasty wee midget, I hope she is flown
by ghosts far away and left starving.

I'll curse her offence and teach her a trick,
for her master would give me a whole cask on tick,
but she gripped at the beer an' acted so thick
I hope God takes her out of her station, but quick!

She's a rotten wee boiler with a vitriol mouth;
she showed me the door and insulted me out.
As for her family, I can't say much for that,
but if she married a ghost, she'd bear him a cat.

She's a club-footed hoor, not a woman at all,
with as barren a face as wanders the road.
She'll be a fool, to be sure, till she runs out of fuel
and the stupid bitch probably shites in the gruel.

Going Blind

from the German of Rainer Maria Rilke

She sat at tea, just like the others.
At first it seemed to me, she held
her cup a little differently to the rest.
She smiled once. It almost hurt.

And when, at last, they all departed,
slowly, and in random order
they went through many rooms.
(One spoke and laughed.)
I saw her. She hung behind the rest

absorbed, as one who soon
must face an audience and sing,
and in her eyes, radiant with joy,
light played, as on a pond's surface.

She followed slowly, dawdling along,
as though there were something to surmount
and yet, as though, once it were overcome,
she would no longer walk, so much as fly.

Errigal
from the Irish of Cathal Ó Searcaigh

In those final years
your body stooped and greyed.
Errigal took you,

angled tight limbs around you,
shouldering you skyward sometimes
on the arch of his back.

He greyed your eyes, imagination;
made fierce stone of them; locked
your mind in the vault of a cliff.

Heather bristled your cheeks,
scraw grew in your eyes, lichen
whitened nape and crown and forehead.

Sunset laid to rest a downy light,
enchanted sparks from your quartz
face, the granite of your brow.

Your words, sharp as scree,
whispered daily down the steep
gradient of your tongue.

Piece by piece he took you,
held you rigid in his ramparts,
commanded you to stay.

But when I see that mountain now,
I see you still, staring from slope and peak
and I know that you have mastered it.

Snow and the Moon
from the Irish of Micheál Ó hAirtnéide

I, alone under the night sky,
kicking gems in a field of snow.
Houses frosted. Every crow's nest
glides like a black moon across the true.
I, dancing alone under the moon,
the ancient dance of the rush of blood;
I am overcome with loneliness—the old loneliness.

There is agony beyond the sky's rim
and death mocks me with
hands rammed in pockets
like a whistling cornerboy.
And I stand in the moonlit snow
and praise the whole crow's-nest shambles,
a poet—arrogant, safe and full of words.

The Well
from the Irish of Cathal Ó Searcaigh

'That'll put the jizz back in you,'
said old Bríd, her eyes glinting,
and she handed me a bowl of real water
from the purest well in Gleann an Átha.
This well, kept sweet and handed down,
was her one family heirloom.
It nestled in a nook, protected,
stonewalled in on all sides,
mouthed by a flagstone.

Here, in the early sixties,
just as I came into my strength,
there wasn't a house in the district
without a well like this. Everyone
so proud of how sweet and cool
they kept their family well. They'd allow
no glut or glar to gather in it
and a trace of rust was reason
enough to bail it out at once with tin
buckets. Each quarter day without
fail, they'd kiln-lime it sweet.

The lucid gush of a true spring
burst and plashed from my people's well.
When we were consumed by thirst
and stuck with summer's sweat
we took it daily by bowl and pawnger.
It slaked and cooled us in fields
and bog. It throbbed through us
like a tonic—gave us life and laughter.
It washed us all, from the infant's
first bath to the corpse's last cleaning.

But for a long time now, there is a snake
of pipe that runs in from the hills,

foreign water in every kitchen in these glens.
Water slops from taps, naked of sparkle,
bitter and strange in the mouth.
We have forgotten our true well.
'It's hard to find a well these days,'
said old Bríd, filling up my bowl again.
'They're hiding in rushes and juking in grass,
all choked up and clatty with scum
but for all the neglect they get
their old mettle is still true.
Look for your own well, pet,
for there's a hard time coming.
It's time to go back to the source.'